Not all teas are created equal

A MingCha Guide to Premium Chinese Tea

This little handbook is intended to be a guide for Chinese tea selection and preparation for those who care about the difference of a premium tea. As our civilization evolves on in an accelerating pace, and everything comes in ready to serve, the experience of real tea is more necessary for us to get in touch with the idea of living.

The complex, millennium old living tradition of tea is a very large body of knowledge. I am trying to share it in a selective, abridged and contemporary language. Hopefully these concepts and ideas can help the readers with additional gains in tea appreciation. The wisdom, the art and the personal gains in the experience will hopefully come in naturally.

I choose to use a very factual and practical language rather than a decorated or cultural tone; I believe a lot of the readers need straight plain information and are capable of making personal observation on their own.

There are ideas and facts in this book that have not been easily accessible by the public and I hope they can be shared by the veterans as well as the novice. That way, we can all see new dimensions and possibilities in the tea experience.

To good life.

W9-BXM-567

Acknowledgements

It was Jackie and Nancy Wan who rode 6 hours and spent two days taking me to their connection in Chaozhou that initiated me to working directly with people of the farms. Without them half-forcing me into this mode of practice, I could have still been trading in a remote way. I could not have related to tea the way I do.

Some information in this book represents my interpretation of the generous teaching and ideas by the many friends and associates in production and research facilities in China. I have to especially mention Guo Xuan, De Huai, Zhuang Yong, and Sibo Ruen, who introduced to me all the reality and practical approaches in tea making. They continue to be my great resources for working level information, which lends an important dimension for the understanding of the mountains of publications on the subject, popular or professional.

The present writing is quite different from its original manuscript, which was initially translated into Japanese by Au Tunglin in Tokyo. The many midnight international calls and lengthy e-mails with her scrutiny of the concepts and details were important inspiration for the rebirth of this writing.

Bobby Lee took the first few photos for free for the MingCha photo stock. It was his invaluable supports that excited me to pick up the camera again to build up the image collections, many of which illustrated these pages.

Another photo contributor is Fei Li, who also produced the artwork for printing. Her dedication to this project reflects more behind the scene in the many late evenings and weekends in the studio or in front of the 21-inch computer monitor. Sam Wong helped me with some of the tea production location shots.

In the background are also Vanessa, Kit Bing and Angelina Bruce. It could have taken at least half a year more to see this book in print if I did not have their dedication in coordination and daily supports.

From the first day I took on promoting Chinese tea, it has been Vivian's unrestrained commitment that make all the achievement possible. Her ideas, sensibility in art, production execution and management efforts are essential to make this book happen. She continues to inspire me for the many projects ahead. It is difficult to imagine my daily work without her.

Leo Kwan
July 2001

Introduction

About Fine Chinese Tea

Unlike the dim sum restaurant tea or the "English" black tea that most people are accustomed to, fine Chinese teas are non-blended, selectively harvested teas of origins and authentic tea plants. Each tea has a distinctive individual taste brought out naturally from the tea leaves and production method. No additives, natural or artificial, should be used.

a green tea
(Longjin)

an oolong tea
(Teguanyin
Light)

a black tea
(Tippy Puer)

a red tea
(Tanyang
Golden Rim)

a yellow tea
(Yellow Needles)

a white tea
(White Peony
Supreme)

Fresh picks are laid for sun-withering for oolong production.

Fine Chinese teas are categorized by the production method into these six main families: greens, oolongs, reds, blacks, whites, and yellows. Each family is subdivided into various subgroups or types by variations in production methods, tea plants and origins. Out of the maze of these hundreds of variations, I shall focus in this book the oolongs, for the obvious reasons of its distinctive characters and great spectrum in taste and health contributing nature. Fine oolongs are, up to this day, products of labour devotion and passion for perfection.

I shall also include some representations from the other tea families that I think are fine enough to put besides the oolongs and are also distinctive enough to be learned and understood.

Chinese tea is a very large body of learning. This little handbook will serve only to give sufficient background information to help the reader to select and prepare tea properly. This is very much needed due to the confusion in the tea market where products of varying natures and price ranges have been carrying the same name. I'd like to encourage even those people who have been consuming fine teas for many years to compare the ideas in this book with what they are used to. Then seek out the products that really match up the ideas. It is my intention that the true quality of what some of the popular tea names describe be more popularly understood and asked for.

As the Occident discovered the wonders of tea centuries ago in the Cathay of China, they eventually had to choose the cheaper mass production options for production, storage, shipping, packaging and obvious commercial concerns in those days, sacrificing the varieties, taste and health benefits. In an era when almost the whole world is just one e-mail or second day delivery away, this ancient decision seems all too irrelevant. It is about time we experience the genuine and even better developed quality, by accessing a global market which supply has been made convenient by the technology today.

What Are Oolongs?

The oolongs are a family of tea characterized by a partial fermentation process that is controllably stopped by heat. It has the benefits and tastes of both the green and the fully fermented teas.

Some of the oolongs are so very lightly partial fermented that they are somewhat like green tea. One example is the original Teguanyin Supreme. Some are more fermented and have a balanced salutary content makeup, such as the Phoenix line. Some have charcoal finishes that our European customers refer to as their morning coffee substitutes, such as the Wuyi line. Some people would even age this kind of teas for 3 years or more; they prefer the mellow taste and aroma, and the milder nature that is friendlier to weaker stomachs.

The original Chinese characters for the word "oolong" are two words, romanized as oo- and -long. The first one means "black" and the second one "dragon". The two words together, besides meaning a "black dragon" which describes the shape of the original oolong tea leaves, is also a colloquial expression for a "careless mistake"; an oolong is like a

mistake, it is not green nor fermented.

Oolongs, whether Teguanyins, Wuyis or Phoenixes, are popular for connoisseurs all over the world for their full spectrum in tastes and versatility for infusion possibilities. In Fujian, Guangdong, Taiwan and Hong Kong, where real tea lovers enjoy tea using tiny teapots and cups in the gungfu infusion tradition, oolongs are the basic as well as supreme choice.

Right: An infused oolong leaf. Notice the reddish color on the edge; this is the part of the leaf that is fermented. Top left: The tea master massages the leaves in 1.5~2 hours intervals throughout the night in production seasons. Left: the Chinese characters for oo- and -long, Below left: a teguanyin style dry leaf and an original style dry leaf.

Traditionally, high quality oolongs have been produced majorly in 3 areas: Northern Guangdong (the Phoenix line), Southern Fujian (the Teguanyin line), and Western Fujian (the Wuyi line). Their prime production are covered in this book. Today, Taiwan also produces some fine oolongs, I shall cover them in later publications as a separate collection. Tea farms in India are also experimenting now, and I look forward to including their successful results in my selections.

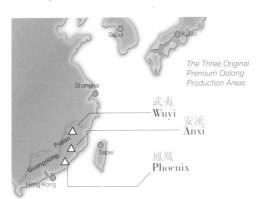

The Three Original Premium Oolong Production Areas

武夷
Wuyi

安溪
Anxi

鳳凰
Phoenix

Good premium teas are sometimes harvested from very old tea bushes like this 500-years "Zilan".

Tea Selection Guide

Teguanyin Supreme

Origin:

Western Anxi, Fujian, China

Production:

Two selective harvests: April~May
(Spring) and October~November
(Fall) from the leaf buds and 2nd
and 3rd leaves. Occassional
partial leaf stalks including.
Leaves should be young but
half open. Multiple hand-turned
partial-fermentation for 8~10 hours.
3 rounds hand-rolled.
Low-temperature set-finished.
No additives.

Character:

High and delicious orchid perfume.
Full, silky body of very light colour
infusion; Light, fresh, crisp, and
clean flavour. Sweet after-taste.

Effects:

Relaxing. Cooling of excessive
body heat and quenching of the
difficult thirst. Antiphlogistic.
Body-cleansing. Antioxidant.
Diuretic. Lowering of blood
cholesterols and other fatty acids.

清香極品 鉄観音

The original Teguanyin is characterized by its high orchidy fragrance, silky texture, full body infusion and thick leaves of rich tea oils. The tea plants grow slowly to such character only in the high mountains of Anxi County in Fujian Province. People have tried to transplant the species elsewhere in other tea plantations, but have never been able to come up with anything close to the original.

Teguanyin Supreme should be masterfully hand-processed and finished to excellence in the perfumy light style the locals prefer. The clear, bright and fragrant infusion is a medium of retreat for the body and soul. Its extremely light impression but slow and steady lingers have made it a tea for meditation. It should be reserved for the

special moment for your special tea companions or just for yourself, to be sipped through the senses in a clean, quiet environment.

It is also the kind of tea that would take a little experiment and practice to infuse. Allow yourself some time for the opportunity to understand the very delicate but supreme tea experience.

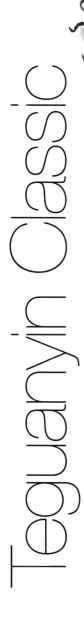

Teguanyin Classic

Origin:

Western Anxi, Fujian, China

Production:

Two selective harvests: April~May (Spring) and October~November (Fall) from the leave buds and 2nd and 3rd leaves. Leaves should be young but half open. Multiple hand-turned partial-fermentation for 8~10 hours. 3 rounds hand-rolled. Slow charcoal fire finish. No additives.

Character:

Clean, fresh smells of early morning woods. Warming aroma. Smooth, brisk and strong infusion with good tone of the orchid fragrance. Quenching after-taste.

Effects:

Refreshing. Revivifying. Body-cleansing. Warming. Freshening of the palate after meals. Lowering of blood cholesterols and other fatty acids.

古方

鉄観音

Like Teguanyin Supreme, the Classic version starts with premium quality picks in the mountains in Anxi County, Fujian. It is as carefully processed except that it is given one more step of charcoal finishing fire. This has been done for a century now for a good reason — to neutralize the cooling energy of the tea plant so that the tea can be consumed throughout the whole day without off-balancing the fire energy of the human body.

The firing, however, has to be light enough not to kill the after-taste fragrance that characterized Teguanyin. It is also very important that the tea would not be overloaded with "fast-heat" energy that could also upset the body energy balance.

Teguanyin Classic has a warming aroma and added depth in taste due to the browning. It is a safer tea for the weaker stomachs or for larger quantity consumption. It can be stored properly for maturity. It can also be used as an expert's tea for extra-strong gungfu infusion — "teguanyin expresso" as it is sometimes referred to.

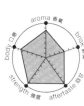

Teguanyin Light

Origin:

Western Anxi, Fujian, China

Production:

Two selective harvests: April~May (Spring) and October~November (Fall) from 2nd and 3rd leaves. Leaves should be young but half open. Multiple hand-turned partial-fermentation for 8~10 hours. 3 rounds hand-rolled. Low-temperature set-finished. No additives.

Character:

With the crisp and refreshing fragrance like that of Chinese orchid after rain. Smooth, crisp, light but strong infusion. Sweet after-taste.

Effects:

Relaxing. Body-cleansing. Antioxidant. Lowering of blood cholesterols and other fatty acids. Cooling of excessive body heat and quenching of the difficult thirst. Antiphlogistic.

芳香鉄観音

A partially fermented, tightly rolled tea originated 260 years ago and has become the most popular of all oolongs, Teguanyins is also the most imitated tea. Quasi-herbal additives and flavouring are commonly used to disguise the look-alikes. Some are even highly priced.

Genuine Teguanyin Light should be naturally processed to a balance for its orchidy fragrance and taste from strictly selected harvests in the origin and laurel seat of the legendary tea — Western Anxi, Fujian. Fermentation should be strong enough to allow for the distinctive

Teguanyin taste character. The reddish brown patches on the jigsaw edge of the infused leaves are good visual evidence.

For people who prefer lighter tastes, Teguanyin Light is more economical than the supreme variety as a regular drink. Those with excessive body heat can use this to calm the energy, cool the system and refresh the mind.

Teguanyin Light is a fine choice for the gourmets, and a friendly selection for the novice — results by various approaches and tryouts are pleasing.

Phoenix Supreme

Origin:

Wudong, Phoenix Mountains, Chao An, Guangdong, China

Production:

Two selective harvests: April~May (Spring) and October~November (Winter) from 2nd and 3rd leaves. Leaves should be young but half open. Multiple hand-turned partial-fermentation for 8~10 hours. Longitudinally twisted. Multiple-low temperature set-finished for the bright variation and medium temperature for the classic (browned) style. Separate-batch-process from individual harvests of matured trees of same ancestry. No additives.

Character:

Round, sweet fruity fragrance. Brisk, smooth and complex infusion. Light clear colour. Refreshing, quenching and sweet after-taste.

Effects:

Relaxing. Revivifying. Facilitate digestion and urination. Mucus and cough reduction. Lowering of blood cholesterols and other fatty acids. Cooling of excessive body heat and quenching of the difficult thirst. Antiphlogistic.

極品 鳳凰單樅

Phoenix Supreme is selectively handpicked from the famous Wudong peak of the Phoenix Mountain in the north of the Guangdong Province, 1,400 meters above sea-level, where the soil, moisture, sun amount, and clean air give the plant its character. These are teas of single-bush thorough propagation from renowned specimens, some dating back as far as the Sung Dynasty (circa 10th-13th century A.D.). There are six major bush types, within each of which the taste can still vary due to the exact location of the plantation and finishing styles.

The leaves are processed in small batches, involving multiple steps of masterly rattling of the

leaves for controlled fermentation, taking place through the very night after the leaves are picked and sun-withered.

The real quality of Phoenix Supreme used to be known only amongst the extremely privileged, even three~four decades ago. Controlled propagation has made these quality commercially possible only recently to allow a larger public to experience the authentic taste.

Phoenix Sung Special

Origin:

Phoenix Mountain, Chao An, Guangdong, China

Production:

Two selective harvests: April~May (Spring) and October~November (Winter) from 2nd and 3rd leaves. Leaves should be young but almost fully open. Harvested from matured trees of the same ancestry. Multiple hand-turned partial-fermentation for 8~10 hours. Longitudinally twisted. Multiple-low temperature set-finished for the bright variation and medium temperature for the classic (browned) style. No additives.

Character:

Sweet flowery or fruity fragrance (depending on the tea variation). The brisk taste can also range from bitter-sweet to fruity-sweet. Light clear colour. Refreshing, quenching and sweet after-taste.

Effects:

Relaxing. Revivifying. Facilitate digestion and urination. Mucus and cough reduction. Lowering of blood cholesterols and other fatty acids. Cooling of excessive body heat and quenching of the difficult thirst. Antiphlogistic.

鳳凰宋種單欉

A tea rolled lengthwise and by very careful partial fermentation, Phoenix Sung Special starts with straight isolated processing of selective hand-picked leaves from the reputable descendants of Sung Dynasty specimens. Different bush types are characterized by various unique sweet fragrance and tastes. Even the dry leaves and infusion colours are different in some species. For example, the famous Phoenix Golden is yellowish brown and gives golden yellow infusion, whereas Honey Orchid's dark dry leaves yield clear light infusion.

The light style finish yields higher fragrance while the classic (browned) style gives depth to the taste. The characteristic brisk fresh tastes can be matured for greater depth in the browned version. All variations work well on the throat.

Phoenix Sung Specials are much closer to wild tea in herbal nature and effects. Some variations even maintain a fresh bitterness similar to the ancient plant.

aroma 香氣
brisk 新鮮
aftertaste 回甘
strength 強度
body 口感

Mandarin Orchid

Origin:

Phoenix Mountain, Chao An, Guangdong, China

Production:

Two selective harvests: April~May (Spring) and October~November (Winter) from 2nd and 3rd leaves. Leaves should be young but almost fully open. Multiple hand-turned partial-fermentation for 8~10 hours. Longitudinally twisted. Multiple-low temperature set-finished for the bright variation and medium temperature for the classic (browned) style. No additives.

Character:

Flowery, honey sweet fragrance. Light colour infusion, clean but fresh and sharp taste. Lingering fragrant and refreshing sensations.

Effects:

Relaxing. Revivifying. Facilitate digestion and urination. Mucus and cough reduction. Lowering of blood cholesterols and other fatty acids. Cooling of excessive body heat and quenching of the difficult thirst. Antiphlogistic.

芝蘭 水仙

Mandarin Orchid is a class of the Phoenix tea family that has a very charming flowery fragrance brought out from within the natural tea leaves during processing. Fire and fermentation has to be balanced in order to bring out the best in its taste without affecting the pleasing aroma.

Fine Phoenix teas, such as Mandarin Orchid, are readily distinguishable for their thicker body, high perfumes and sharper tastes. They are enjoyed throughout Chao An county and in the city of Chaozhou, where tea infusion has sublimated to become an art form as well as a daily routine. Whether the small dark sticks are infused in tiny Chinese lid-cups or the nectarine size gungfu clay pots, or in fine bone china in the hotel, Phoenix teas are enjoyed in all corners in this city of tea. It is not an exaggeration to say where there is people, there is tea, and infused throughout the whole day.

Mandarin Orchid is priced aggressively low by MingCha to allow for an easy entry point to experience the world of Phoenix oolongs.

Wuyi Supreme

Origin:

Wuyi Mountains, Fujian, China

Production:

April~May harvest of 2nd and 3rd open young leaves from controlled propagation of matured trees from same ancestry. Multiple hand-turned partial fermentation for 10~14 hours. Multiple fire set with longitudinal twisting. Charcoal finished. No additives.

Character:

Sweet aroma of the flower of osmanthus with a suggestion of warm charcoal. Round, full-body. Malty, brisk, fresh taste and quenching after-taste.
Can be further matured under proper storage.

Effects:

Slow warming energy for the body. High soluble contents including polyphenols. Polyphenols are associated as an anti-ageing, anti-oxidation agent. Can be used as a pacifying treat for calming down the morning or the afternoon rush.

極
品

武
夷
紅
袍

The history of Wuyi as a prime tea production area started as way back as the 9th century, embroidered with romantic poems and imperial praises. "Bohea" (from the local dialect for Wuyi), as it was called in those days by the Europeans, was once referred to as "black tea" because of its colour difference from the green tea. After it had been introduced to the privileged class in the seventeenth century, it soon overtook green tea as the major import until Chinese fully fermented tea (red tea) started to dominate in 1840s.

The mystic, rocky cliffs of the Wuyi Mountains remain to this day the mecca of oolong tea. The tea produced in this area is specifically called Yán Cha, or "Tea of the Rock". My supreme

choice is produced from the propagation of the legendary and highest regarded of all Wuyi teas, the Red Cloak (Da Hung Pao).

As with all Wuyi tea, the "Red Cloak" is even better brewed in a Yixing teapot, especially when the tea is not aged. The special teaware enhances the characteristic rich aroma and taste of the tea, and plays down the heat energy of the fire. The "Red Cloak" can be matured if preferred.

Cassia Supreme

Origin:

Wuyi Mountains, Fujian, China

Production:

April~May harvest of 2nd and 3rd open young leaves of matured trees of improved species of the ancient plant. Multiple hand-turned partial fermentation for 10~14 hours. Multiple fire set with longitudinal twisting. Charcoal finished. No additives.

Character:

Sweet aroma of the cassia bark (the reason for the tea name) with a suggestion of warm charcoal. Smooth, mellow, malty taste and quenching after-taste. Suitable for further maturing under proper storage.

Effects:

Slow warming energy for the body. High in polyphenols content. Polyphenols are associated as an anti-ageing, anti-oxidation agent. The aged version is an appropriate tea for the weaker stomach.

武夷 貢品玉桂

Possibly the first oolong, teas from Wuyi have enjoyed an extremely high reputation. The aromatic and brisk, malty infusion possesses also the fragrant and sharp character of fine, greener oolongs. Like all reputable traditional Wuyi Rock Teas, the Cassia is made with multiple steps of interlaced low-fire and fermentation.

A French customer once referred to this tea as her substitution for coffee during breakfast. The fire finish does give the tea a charcoal-roasted result. The trick, however, lies in the balance, where the delicate flavour associable with the bark of the cassia tree is still maintained and the texture is still smooth and not charred.

Wuyi Cassia is critically acclaimed for its complex depth of flavours and authenticity of origin and production environment. It is a tea loved by the connoisseurs and easily understandable by the novice. The matured version is mellow (which some connoisseurs would prefer), while the newer tea tastes brighter. Both can be further matured with proper conditions and care.

Wuyi Dark Rock

Origin:
Wuyi Mountains, Fujian, China

Production:
April~May harvest of 2nd and 3rd open young leaves from the hybrid prunes of renowned individual tea plants. Multiple hand-turned partial fermentation for 10~14 hours. Multiple fire set with longitudinal twisting.
Charcoal finished. No additives.

Character:
Warm aroma of the cassia bark with a suggestion of warm charcoal. Smooth, mellow, malty taste and quenching after-taste. Suitable for further maturing under proper storage.

Effects:
Slow warming energy for the body. High in polyphenols content. Polyphenols are associated as an anti-ageing, anti-oxidation agent. Maturing can make this tea friendlier to the weaker stomachs than green or red teas.

武夷正岩水仙

One staple tea in the dim sum restaurant is Shui Xian. Although hardly the authentic thing now, the tea is still extremely popular. It is easier for one to trace the reason with a sip of the original version: a warming aroma of the charcoal finish and a nutty, substantial infusion make this tea almost ideal as a wake-up drink to accompany the small but heavy dishes.

Wuyi Shui Xian, as it was originally called, is the variety that once dominated the majority of oolong consumption. It refers to the family of tea produced using the Wuyi oolong method with the local plants. There are hundreds of varieties, amongst them the extremely well-known Da Hung Pao and Cassia. Shui Xian can be extremely exquisite two-kilos-a-year production or the low-land economical versions. Only those planted alongside the big, dark

rocks lining the steep mountains are the original and authentic ones, and are often referred to as Yán-Cha (tea from the rock).

Wuyi Dark Rock is a premium Shui Xian for enjoying the same warm aroma and distinctive flavour that once charmed princes and queens all over the world.

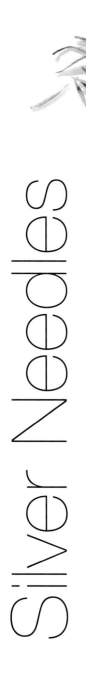

Silver Needles

Origin:

Zhenghe-Fuding area, Northern Fujian, China

Production:

First flush of the "Dai-bai" tea tree young downy buds. Single-layer air dried with or without the aid of extremely low heat (depending on weather) for 2~3 days. Naturally partial fermented. Low heat set-finished. Non-turned, non-rolled. No additives.

Character:

Fragrant dry leaves and infusion. Mellow but fresh. Delicate, smooth and soothing taste. Tea in its most natural and pristine form. Nice visual effects when brewed in the tall glass.

Effects:

Cooling of body heat. Purification of the blood pertaining to the effects of abnormal body heat. Antiphlogistic. Anti-oxidizing. Diuretic. Contains substances that retard growth of cancer cells and tissue mutation.

極品

白毫銀針

Throughout its history, Silver Needles has been adorned not only for its taste, aroma and health benefits, but also for its appearance. It has been a much sought after rare tea for centuries. Just the plucking process alone is a challenge: breaking the tippy little bud from the leaf stalks without flattening the silvery down lining the bud surface. The withering, fermentation and drying processes that follow are even more difficult to master. The production of genuine Silver Needles has been uniquely Chinese and the volume has been very limited.

Good Silver Needles should be produced from tea bushes selected for the taste and health benefits in the high misty mountains of Northern Fujian, rather than for the fine silver hair appearance alone. Recent researches with Silver Needles have shown evidence of higher efficient combination of polyphenols and other health contributing components, suggesting that it may be more effective than green and oolong teas in anti-oxidation and anti-mutation of the body cells. Most important for the connoisseurs, however, fine Silver Needles is an unique enjoyment to the senses.

White Peony Supreme

Origin:

Zhenghe-Fuding area, Northern Fujian, China

Production:

First to second flush of the "Dai-bai" tea tree young hairy buds and first leaves. Single-layer air dried with the aid of extremely low heat for two and a half days. Naturally partial fermented. Low heat set-finished. Non-turned, non-rolled. No additives.

Character:

Fragrant dry leaves and infusion. Mellow but fresh. Malty, smooth and soothing taste.

Effects:

Cooling of body heat. Purification of the blood pertaining to the effects of abnormal body heat. Antiphlogistic. Anti-oxidizing. Diuretic. Contains substances that retard growth of cancer cells and tissue mutation.

高山 白牡丹

Premium white tea is produced with minimal but carefully mastered processing, involving slight and very slow fermentation, and low temperature drying. This is to keep the tea's own pristine nature, while bringing out its best taste and fragrance. The cooling effect of the plant can thus be maintained, making it salutary to those with higher body heat.

It is worth noting that some farms do produce look-alikes using heat to quickly dry the leaves to save production resources. The results are totally different from the characteristic, pleasant tastes of white teas.

Genuine White Peony is a light and good all-day drink. A little honey can be mixed into the infused liquid if preferred, but preparing it well and enjoying it

plain is most rewarding. It is also a very friendly tea for casual consumption — as long as the water temperature is observed, infusion is almost care free and good result is easily achieved. The characteristics of this tea is most obvious when it is aged for 1~2 years.

X'tra Old Tippy Puer

Origin:

Si Mao Area, Yunnan, China

Production:

Wok-fry withering of young leaves and buds of a local Yunnan species. Rolled and heat-set before hydro-piled-fermentation. Den-matured. No additives.

Character:

Earthy, woody aroma. Full body, mellow, smooth and strong taste. Infusion colour varies from clear dark amber to rich dark burgundy with easy control. Strength can vary dramatically without bitterness.

Effects:

Lowering of blood fatty acids. Helps in weight control. Aids digestion and regularity. Reliefs alcohol intoxication. Regulates internal osmosis. Due to its more neutral character, a safer tea for the weaker stomachs.

Special storage:

Further ageing possible when stored properly in a covered, porous container in a dry, ventilated environment, cool and away from the sun.

特級珍藏 金尖普洱

The Puer I am introducing here is very different from the coarse leaf varieties usually seen in the market. A fine quality Puer should start with selection of prime young tea leaves from the southwest remote highlands of the Yunnan Province, and through carefully conditioned ageing in the dens at the farms. The tea leaves should be small and even in size, clean and clear brown in colour. The more matured the tea is, the cleaner is the smell of the dry leaves. The infusion yields a smoother, fuller liquor.

Extremely fine Puers like this can be infused with a dramatically wide range of strength while maintaining its mellow and smooth characters, and without bitterness. They are fine alternatives to thousand-dollar genuine old Puer cakes for the taste and effectiveness. It is a good option for the senior, the weaker stomachs and the weight-watchers for its neutralizing, degreasing, and system-cleansing effects, while maintaining its mild character.

Tanyang Golden Rim

Origin:

Fu-on area, Northern Fujian, China

Production:

Second flush (early Spring but usually after Ching Ming, for strength in taste) harvest of young tippy "Fu-yun 7" (a prune-improved species in the 80's of the traditional variety) tea plants. 8~12 hours air withered. Fully rolled for fermentation. Medium fire heat set. No additives.

Character:

Sweet, fruity aroma. Fresh, smooth taste. Strength adjustable according to preference. Sweet after-taste. May be enjoyed with milk, honey, lemon or spices; or can be infused using gungfu infusion method and sipped in its pure form. Can be served chilled.

Effects:

Revivifying. Aids in digestion and lowering of blood pressure.

坦
洋
工
夫
紅

Tanyang was just a tiny tea village in the mountains of northern Fujian province 150 years ago, when a native by the name of Wu made a fermented tea that sold so popularly in Europe that by the end of that century, the one kilometer main street was jammed with 36 tea trading companies, exporting more than 1.5 million kilograms a year. The tree plantation and production process have now been further improved to produce Tanyang Gungfu*, which some people in the trade have given it a fancy name of "Golden Hair Monkey".

Premium Tanyang Gungfu yields a liquor of clear amber colour with a bright golden rim on the surface. That is why I refer to it as Tanyang Golden Rim. It is a very versatile tea adaptable in various infusion and preparation approaches,

hot or chilled, and can even be seasoned with spices, honey, lemon or dairy cream. I think it is best, however, when enjoyed as is.

* The Chinese phrase "Gungfu" means industrious efforts. The tea has been referred to as Tanyang Gungfu due to the great amount of manual skills and efforts needed for producing the tea.

First Flush Longjin

Origin:
Si Ming Mountains,
Zhejiang Province, China

Production:
Hand-plucked first flush (early
Spring before Ching Ming Festival)
young leaf buds of cross-pruned
matured local tea plants.
Approximately seventy thousand
plucks to each kilo of dry leaves.
8~10 hours shaded withered.
Two times hand-pressed low
temperature wok fried.
No additives.

Character:
Warm, malty aroma. Crisp,
sharp taste. Cooling after taste on
sides of the tongue.

Effects:
Revivifying. Aids in digestion and
lowering of blood pressure.
Anti-oxidizing. Anti-cholesterol
build up.

明前龍井

The warming, malty character of Longjin is a reflection of the lengthy wok-fry production process, which gives a balance of heat energy to the early spring cool mist of the mountain air and the sharp chilly underground water that nourish the famous tea plant.

Good productions always have to be hand-fried (the worker actually uses the hand as the tool) for better control of the taste and appearance quality. It is a highly skilled and tedious process. Although a very big wok is used, the workers have to start each batch with only 100 grams of fresh leaves each time!

Longjin is best infused for individual consumption in the tall glass or the porcelain lid-cup, such that each person can

control his or her own pace and replenish the infusion with water at the right time. In decanting, always keep one third of the liquid in the infusion ware for the next round of infusion. Have patience to infuse for the proper duration for the full taste. Then you will understand why it is the most popular and well-known green tea in China.

What's In The Chop?

Since my selection of MingCha teas is small estate produced and is harvest specific, it is important that the customers are well informed of the background of the products. In addition to the regular production information printed on the packages or labels, there is a coloured chop on each pack specifying the bush type and harvest season. In cases where detailing of a location or finishing style is not covered in print, the chop also supplements the information. Origins, bush types, harvest seasons and finishing styles do all contribute to taste differences in the leaves.

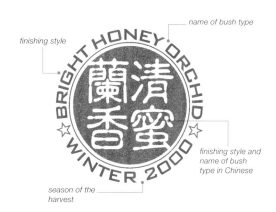

finishing style

name of bush type

finishing style and name of bush type in Chinese

season of the harvest

detail location name

name of bush type

detail location name and bush type in Chinese

season of the harvest

Infusion Guide

Introduction

Fine tea is like a fine food ingredient, it has to be properly prepared in order to deliver its best taste.

Luckily, preparing a fine cup of tea is easier than mastering fine cooking. I have outlined some general basic concepts and specific requirements for each tea group for the readers to have a foundation to start off. Two major schools of tea preparation, the conventional and the gungfu approaches are covered. For people who like fine Chinese green or white teas, I am proposing the mainstream tall glass approach.

Like cooking, tea infusion has to be practised to be good. To me, it has always been a light-hearted and relaxing process. The tea experience, after all, can be very personal or social, meditative or celebrative. I hope it is always enjoyable to you.

Basic Concept

General speaking, the less tea with more water gives you milder infusion and vice versa. The strength of the infusion also increases as the infusion time increases.

With the exception of premium white and green teas, all premium quality Chinese teas should yield pleasing results with either the conventional method — a "spoonful" of tea to a cup of water, or the expert preferred "gungfu" approach. However, due to the difference in leaf density, production method and finishing, all teas vary a bit in optimum temperature, tea-water ratio and infusion time. Personal preference and difference in the concept of a "good infusion" are also key factors in deciding for yourself what is the best for you. I recommend that you start by referring to the following suggestion and fine-tune an approach you are most happy with.

If it is possible, do try and explore the gungfu approach. Once you have your first success, you'll continue to fine new levels of enjoyment and understand why it is the preferred method for so many tea lovers.

Conventional Approach

Put the recommended amount of tea into pot. Half fill the pot with water at the recommended temperature.

Cover the lid, rock the pot in a circular direction to warm up the pot and rinse the tea. Empty and discard the liquid. These two steps should be done in 20 seconds or less. *(In case of gungfu reds, extremely fine whites and greens, just preheat the pot alone.)*

Fill the pot again with water at the recommended temperature. Cover and infuse for the right duration. Decant into cups, leaving no liquid in the pot. Serve while hot.

Tall Glass Approach

For premium white and green teas

Method 1: **Surface drop**
(for denser leaves)
Warm glass. Fill glass with water. Drop tea onto the water surface and let it gradually soak up and sink to the bottom.

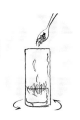

Method 2: **Sandwich drop**
(lighter and denser leaves)
a) Warm glass. Fill 1/3 of glass with water. Drop tea onto the water. Swirl the mixture by turning the glass one or two rounds. Let soak for 1/2 to 3/4 of the infusion time.

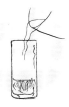

b) Add water to fill the glass and infuse for the remains of the duration.

Infusion in a tall plain glass is intended for watching the readiness of the infusion and admiring the movement of fine tea leaves. You can serve right out of the glass or decant into smaller glasses. If you do not have a tall glass, use any small teapots in which the leaves can flow freely.

Gungfu Approach

The basic idea of infusing in the Gungfu Approach is to get the best taste and aroma effects from the tea, basing on the employment of certain teaware and procedure. The characteristic small quantity has its historic linkage to professional and high society tea tasting/competition, and is important to maintain a reasonable pace for in-depth tea enjoyment. The quality of the tea, therefore, has to be good enough for you to spend the little extra time to go through this approach. Allow yourself some playful spirit and opportunities to explore and improve on it, any change in the variables: tea, water, quantity, time, temperature, ware quality and even the way you handle these things, can result in different effects. Once mastered, you would not have tea any other ways.

Put the recommended amount of tea on a piece of white paper. (The amount can be varied according to personal preference.)

Heat teapot with water* at the recommended temperature. Empty pot.

Teaware may be burning hot now, please handle with care.

Put tea into pot. Slowly fill pot with water at the recommended temperature.

While covering the lid, skim away surface foam on the tea.

Empty water from pot into the cups to warm the cups.

You will need these basic things to start with:

- A genuine Yixing pot, around 150 ml capacity.
  (You may substitute this with a Chinese style lid-cup.)
- Small tea cups.
- A bigger cup/flask for holding extra infusion.
- A tray to hold the spilling during infusion
  and decantation.
- A thin chopstick for clearing the pot spout.
- A small electric kettle with easy on-off control.
- A towel.
- A bowl for discarding tea-warming water.
- A jar for fresh water.
- Some people may also need a timer.
- A clean piece of paper with no smell to hold
  the leaves.
- Your favourite fine tea.

Fill pot again with water. Brew for the recommended duration. Strength of tea can be adjusted with duration, but do not exceed the recommended time.

While brewing, empty cups and arrange them adjacent to, and touching one another on a tray or on a tea boat.

Pour brewed tea into cups, starting with a little for each cup, then continuously going round the cups. Tea flow should be consistent and nonstop until pot is empty.

In case there is more content in the pot than the cups can hold, empty content into a bigger pre-warmed cup for serving later. Do not leave tea liquid in the pot after infusion.

Let cool down a little, relax and enjoy.

Infusion Variables According To Tea Type

Conventional Approach:

Legend: 🥄 Tea amount   1 teaspoonful of tea   half tablespoonful of tea   1 tablespoonful of tea   ▲ increase time by about 30% each time

Tea type	Tea amount to water ratio		Temperature	Initial infusion time	Number of infusion
	Tea amount	Water amount			
Teguanyin Supreme			90°C	1 to 4 minutes (optimum:2 min. 30 sec.)	2 ▲
Teguanyin Light			92°C	1 to 4 minutes (optimum:1 min. 30 sec.)	2 ▲
Teguanyin Classic		150ml	92°C	1 to 5 minutes (optimum:3 min.)	3 ▲
Phoenix Supreme			85°C	30 seconds to 3 minutes (optimum:1 min. 15 sec.)	2 ▲
Phoenix Sung Special			85°C	30 seconds to 3 minutes (optimum:1 min.)	2 ▲
Mandarin Orchid		150ml	90°C	30 seconds to 3 minutes (optimum:1 min.)	2 ▲
Wuyi Supreme			92°C	30 seconds to 3 minutes (optimum:2 min.)	2 ▲
Wuyi Dark Rock			95°C	30 seconds to 3 minutes (optimum:2 min.)	2 ▲
Cassia Supreme		150ml	95°C	30 seconds to 3 minutes (optimum:2 min.)	2 ▲
Golden Tip Puer			100°C	1 to 5 minutes (optimum:2 min.)	1 ▲
Tanyang Golden Rim		150ml	100°C	2 to 5 minutes (optimum:4 min.)	1 ▲

Gungfu Approach:

		Vessel	Temperature	Time (¾ potful of tea)	Infusions * (increase time by about 15% each time)
Teguanyin Supreme			90°C	1 minute	6 △
Teguanyin Light			92°C	30 seconds to 1 minute	6 △
Teguanyin Classic		150ml *	92°C	30 seconds to 2 minutes	7 △
Phoenix Supreme			85°C	15 to 45 seconds	5 △
Phoenix Sung Special			90°C	10 to 45 seconds	5 △
Mandarin Orchid		150ml *	90°C	25 seconds to 2 minutes	4 △
Wuyi Supreme			92°C	25 seconds to 2 minutes	6 △
Wuyi Dark Rock			95°C	20 seconds to 2 minutes	6 △
Cassia Supreme		150ml *	95°C	20 seconds to 2 minutes	4 △
Golden Tip Puer			100°C	15 seconds to 3 minutes	4 △
Tanyang Golden Rim		150ml *	100°C	15 seconds to 2 minutes	3 △

Tall Glass Approach:

		Vessel	Temperature	Time	Infusions
White Peony Supreme			80°C	4 minutes or until most leaves sink to the bottom	2
Silver Needle Supreme		150ml	80°C	5 minutes or until most leaves sink to the bottom	2
Longjin			80°C	6 minutes or until most leaves sink to the bottom	3

Notes: ¾ potful of tea   half potful of tea   * average gungfu pot size for big-gungfu-cups   △ increase time by about 15% each time

About Water

Fine teas are especially responsive to the nature of the water used for infusion. The contents of water, such as the minerals and oxygen level, have definite effects on the quality of the infusion.

The ideal water would be that of a very low mineral content soft water or temporary hard water from a spring. In real life situation, I recommend installing a good water filter system or series of systems. Low mineral content bottled water or distilled water can be used if the water in your region is impossibly hard. Always dilute your mineral water and never fully boil it.

Hard water can make your fine tea dark, murky, and chalky in taste. It can also bleach the colour of the leaves, reducing the whole experience. Same thing happens when you use a high mineral content bottled water. In case you have to use such water, keep the temperature on the low side, i.e. never boil it, and keep the infusion time shorter.

Even when an appropriate water is used, avoid repeatedly reheating the same batch of water. Either use up most of each heated batch or dilute it with fresh one. That is another reason why the connoisseurs prefer infusing smaller amount each time for surer and more even control of the temperature.

The emperors of China used to have water for tea carried in from royally appointed water springs, freshly everyday. There was a team of people just responsible for that. Fine well-water, which was readily available in the palaces, was definitely not good enough for his majesty's fine tea. We are actually more lucky than the ancient monarchs for choice of water supply. Not only do we have the access to water from all over the world in the neighbourhood supermarket, but also numerous water treatment and improvement systems readily installable in the average household. If you care enough to get a fine tea, do go the extra mile by experimenting with different water, the results are always amazing.

Teaware

Teaware is an important part of the tea experience not only because of the atmosphere it can create, but also for the infusion effects it plays an essential part in. In this context, I shall focus on the functional aspects in teaware selection rather than the decorative appearance.

Size

Pot size should be determined by the amount of tea it is designed for each round of serving. As described in the infusion tips, the volume should be totally used up in each infusion. So the key factors in determining which pot size you should use are the number of guests and the serving size.

It is always easier to control smaller amount than a larger one. That is why if you think you need to improve your understanding of a new tea or refine your infusion control, start with a smaller size.

Smaller sizes also allow you to serve more rounds with fresher and hotter brews. Your guests and yourself would be able to appreciate better the aroma and taste of a finer tea.

The short-coming of a smaller size is more frequent attention to infusion, and that may be distracting sometimes. The way round it would be to have a set complete with all infusion tools and needs, so that they can be on or near your serving table all the time.

Bigger serving size is good when the best serving temperature of your tea is not high on your priority, and the first impression of the infusion quality is good enough while the bigger cup is still hot. It is appropriate when you are serving a larger crowd or when you are not in the mood to infuse more rounds.

Materials

Materials are essential in that they contribute directly to the effects of your infusion. Genuine Yixing clay is the best material for the teapot. It actually helps to improve the texture, aroma and taste of the infusion. The one shortfall is that there are too many imitations in the market and some may be chemically harmful. Go to a reliable merchant or go for a reputable brand.

Fine china is good that it loses heat very steadily on the outside and reflect heat on the inside to maintain a good infusion temperature. It is relatively care-free and therefore is very convenient. That is why it is the material of choice for most professional tasters. A lot of connoisseurs would also prefer fine china cups even when they are using Yixing pots.

If you prefer thicker material for the tactile effect, go for a high-temperature-fired, no-smell, unglazed and dense ceramic. It is porous and allow for better ventilation of the steam during infusion and therefore does less harm to the tea.

When the visual effect of the infusion itself is a consideration, go for glassware. Glass is also good as cups, as its transparency let you and your guests appreciate the colour of the infusion.

Other materials such as porcelain, silver, stainless steel and glazed iron are usable.

Avoid pewter, aluminium, uncoated iron, plastics, lacquer, and other synthetics, since they easily oxidize and/or emit substances and smell when heated, which even if not harmful, are alien to tea.

Style

Style is mentioned here for its functional purposes. Whatever the shape and form, it is important for the ware to receive the tea leaves and water easily, have enough room for the leaves to spread and flow during infusion and ergonomically shaped for controlled decantation.

The usual shape of the pot for the connoisseur is spherical; tasters use lid cups; fine green tea drinkers prefer a tall glass.

As for the serving cups, the main consideration lies in temperature and vapourization management. A wider top allows easy cool down for more instantaneous sipping. A bigger body holds more fluid for slightly longer heat retention. Tall, thinner shapes tend to pipe out the smell with better efficiency.

Other considerations are personal, cultural and social, which are beyond the intention of coverage in this guidebook.

Opposite page: Yixing pots are treasured for their unrivalled potential to improve infusion quality. Left column top down, then right column, artist name then style name: 1. Lao On Shun, Hand-thrown Shuiping; 2. Anonymous, Tai-li; 3. Hui Mengchen (imitation), Gufu; 4. Wang Shijing, Ai Danbao; 5. Yun-e, Daoba Xishi; 6. Zhou Gengda, Zhujie Duoqiu; 7. Zhou Gengda, Han Yun; 8. Ya Jun, Chi-lian (1935); 9. Wu Guojun, Fan-tai Shuiping; 10. He Yanping, Kuei Hua; 11. Zhang Yanming, Hand-thrown Li-xing; 12. Chen Guo-liang, Yuan-zhu.

About Straining

If you prefer a built-in strainer in the pot, choose those styles that will allow the tea-leaves to expand and free-flow the most. There is a very popular Asian design that is like a small sieve structure on the inside of the pot at the joint with the spout, which I personally prefer. This same idea has been adapted by some international ware brands into their modern designs, which I think is a good idea.

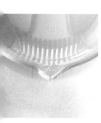

Some make a very large cup-shaped infuser inside the body, which make it easy for you to control the infusion time by simply removing the infuser. I think it is a practical design as long as the size is maximized for the pot and the flow of liquid amongst the leaves is relatively free.

The only other choice is the traditional strainer that you put on top of the cup during decantation. Small infusers, built-in or separate, that allow poor free-flow are not advisable.

The Chinese-design lid cup is preferred by most tasters and professionals around Fujian and Northern Guangdong. The 120ml cup is used as a teapot and the lid serves as a shutter to allow only the liquid to come out during decantation. It is most convenient and efficient, providing that you are willing to invest a little time to learn to use it, and do not mind the extra heat on your fingertips in the beginning. For me as a taster, it is the most convenient tea infusion tool around.

Besides The Tin

Storing of tea is not only a storage issue. It has to do with flavour control and value enhancement, and is tea type specific. We shall look at some basic skills and major concerns in this chapter.

Alien Substances

Grease (such as the natural secretion on your skin), light, oxygen, moisture and alien smell are bad enemies to tea in general. Fine teas are especially fragile and can easily be changed by such elements.

To take out an amount for infusion, always pour the leaves from the container and use up all the portion touched by the hand. If a spoon is needed, use a dry one.

Keep enough portion for daily use for a couple of months in an air-tight container which you can open and close without much hassle. The rest of your stock should be double sealed to minimize air and humidity contact.

Temperature

When the freshness of a tea is an important aspect of its flavour, such as in the case of green teas and fragrant style Teguanyins, keeping the tea after opening for longer than half a year in room temperature without special sealing will result in some loss in flavour. Most official tea books from mainland China suggest storing at 0°C for extending flavour integrity for one year. In practice, I recommend doing it at 9 ± 2°C.

Just make sure that you wrap the tea well for trapping out humidity and odours in the fridge.

NEVER open a pack of tea when it is lower than room temperature. The moisture in the air can easily condense onto the leaves and cause irreversible damage to the flavour. Depending on the pack volume, let stand in room temperature for half a day or until total warm up before opening. That is why it is a good idea to store in the fridge small portion packs and "defrost" one pack per type of tea at a time.

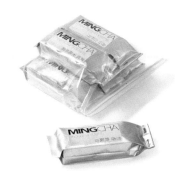

Opposite page: One of the worst enemies for tea is grease. The only time you should touch tea with your hand is before you put it in the pot for infusion.

This page: Separating your stock into smaller portions, say 50 or 100 grams for weekly use and "defrost" them a few at a time.

Most other oolongs and white teas store well for years in a cool shaded area, especially if you want to age them. However, they do maintain their fresh crisp taste at the recommended storage temperature, even a couple of years after harvest.

Choosing Containers

Traditionally, tea was kept tightly wrapped in two layers of natural paper, put into a ceramic container, or bamboo woven container layered with waxed paper, and lined with lime stones.

This is a little too cumbersome for the modern person.

A can that has an air trap, such as the traditional tea can, is most convenient for daily use. Malaysian non-lead pewter cans are very fine. However, if you are more budget conscious like me, use a well-made aluminium or stainless steel can that has good reliable seams (or better yet, no seams) with a good airlock lid. If you think your tea will be in that can for a couple of months before total consumption, use an additional bag inside.

Choose a tea can by examining how fit the two covers are to the body.

One way to determine if the can is well sealed off is to submerge the whole thing, lid facing down, in water. Take it out at least half a day later and dry the outside before opening to check the amount of sip-through. A good one should have very little or no water inside.

Since I have to work with more than a hundred different teas each year, I prefer bags made with a good quality real aluminium laminate that has no smell and is chemically stable for bulk storage, at either room or low temperature. It is light and air-tight and is flexible and economical. It can work easily with another such bag or a Ziploc for added confidence. Or can even be put into a bigger solid container.

A Note On Materials

Most of the time we would think that plastics are good air insulator. The fact is, most plastics have microscopic pores and cannot really work alone effectively. A laminate of two or more layers of different materials increases the effectiveness of air and light insulation. A good aluminium laminate should compose of two layers of different plastics sandwiching a real aluminium sheet. Most of the silvery wrapping materials are electrolytic plastics and are not air or light tight. Hold them to your eyes and look towards the light and you'll understand what I mean. Those that have odours (a lot of plastics do) should not be used.

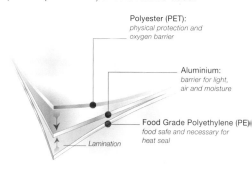

An Effective and Economical Packing and Storage Material.

Pewter, steel, aluminium, glass, ceramics and porcelain are very good storing materials providing that they are clean of any alien materials on the surface and have not been holding another substance with smell.

Maturing Of Tea

Many kinds of tea are not the best when they are fresh. The most well known are the Puers. All good Puers should be matured for at least 5 years before releasing into the market.
Matured Puers can be stored as any other teas or can be further matured by giving it periodical "breathing" time — contact with fresh air in a very shaded area for half a day in dryer weather. Properly aged Puers do taste much better and can fetch comparatively higher price. The Puer cake is known to have been auctioned for tens of thousand US dollars a piece (for about 250 gm).

Puer cakes are just one form of compacting tea for economy in storage and transportation.

Traditional oolongs, notably the Wuyis and the Phoenixes, come to age at least 2 months after production, stored in air-tight condition. It is very popular for people to stored up Wuyis for two to three years, mostly simply in air-tight containers at room temperature. The character of the tea changes through time. The heat from high fire baking is replaced with a mellow warming energy, which works deep into your digestion system.
For people with a fragile body energy balance, I do think that well-aged Wuyis are more suitable than fresh ones. Some old tea shops sell only matured Wuyis. Aged teas, depending on the degree of maturity, are generally more expensive than fresh ones.

To mature tea, start with fresh, dried ones from your reliable dealer. Fully pack your container and make sure everything is double sealed and put the container in a really cool and shaded area. Put a label with a starting date and an intended mature date, together with the tea name, on each container. Two years usually is good enough for most Phoenixes. Three years for Wuyis. Although both can mature for much longer.

When infusing a matured tea, always use hotter water than that for the same tea when fresh. Give it a good wake-up wash before the first infusion. Sometimes it is amazing to see how some dark dry leaves becoming young green again in the first infusion. You can also experiment with a little less leaves and longer infusion time. Matured teas behave a little differently than fresh ones and are always a delight to infuse with.

These are teas that are best at least 2 months after production and can be stored for one year or longer before consumption:
>   The Phoenix, the classic style Teguanyins, the Whites, the Yellows

These are teas that can be stored for maturity:
>   The Wuyis, the Phoenixes, and the Puers

These are teas that are best between one to nine months after production and can be stored in the fridge for more than one year:
>   The fried greens, the light style Teguanyins

These are teas that are best when they are the freshest and should be used up in a year even stored in the fridge:
>   The steamed greens, the pre-finished Phoenixes and Teguanyins.

The Taste of Chinese Tea

The Taste of Chinese Tea

To most of us, tea is something for the food to go down with, or a drink after food.

The domination of European oriented industrialization and trading modes in the past century has vastly changed the popular concept of tea. It is needed for marketing a product with its specific tastes characterized by its industrialized production origin.

Premium Chinese tea has its own evolution path.

Tea originated as a medicine and then a treat in itself. Small pick food was developed afterwards to aid the tea experience. It has further been elevated, not only in China, but also in Japan and Korea, as a major theme for the social, spiritual and cultural experience. Where it has been a

Getting tea from China had not been easy for the Europeans; this boat, loaded with the much sought after import, sank before it could reach its destination in Götheborg, Sweden. That was September, 1745. Even after 1890, when the first operable plantation could export from Assam in the then British colony of India, it still took more than half a year before the product could be in the European consumer's teapot. Far right: Respect of nature is an important guiding principle in Chinese tea making: notice the painstaking keeping of the original leaf form in fine Longjin (a green tea).

daily necessity for the mass, it has also been an object and a ritual for the poets, the monks and the royals, for which a wealthy connoisseur could go bankrupt and a scholar could devote his career.

This evolution has affected tremendously the ideal of the taste of tea and how Chinese tea is rated by certain social groups. Through the centuries, a large proportion of farms have been targeting this kind of taste requirements and continue to develop such markets. Annual competitions amongst these farms and the results become benchmarks and trendsetters.

So what is the taste difference that this kind of evolution has brought about?

Subtlety.

To the untrained or distracted palate, fine Chinese tea is just a delight to the taste buds, a refreshing wash after heavy doses of stimulation.

To the sensitive ones, the finer is always subtly finer in so many ways: the smell and appearance of the dry leaves; the aroma of the liquor; the taste, the texture, and the colour of the infusion; the effects on the palate, the tongue and inside of the cheeks; the sweet after-taste on the throat or in the mouth.... To be able to fully appreciate fine tea, other than all the necessary supplies, one needs to attend to the simple, yet subtly rich experience itself.

Opposite page: 13th century Chinese painting: Tea Competition. Above: A court maid serving tea in the 10th century.

Appreciation of real fine Chinese tea, therefore, is an opportunity to set aside the routines for the small thing of a cup of tea. For that, one gets in touch with the wonders of tea and the delicate senses capable of by the self. This brief moment, no matter one minute or half an hour, because of the relaxing focus that it creates, is an opportunity to feel our own existence and the simple greatness of Nature.

That is why this can easily lend itself to the religious or the spiritual, or even become an art form.

To the majority of us, however, the opportunity for a nice and pacifying break as often as we want it, giving ourselves a brief retreat from the hectic of modernity to enjoy the simple preparation process and subtle fine tastes, is in itself a most entertaining and revivifying daily experience.

Once you are open up to the delicate subtleness of premium Chinese tea, the kaleidoscopic spectrum of tastes and characters can be so much a vast territory to explore and enjoy. Whether you are the cultural, the spiritual, the health conscious, the scientific scholarly, or simply after the great tastes, premium Chinese tea awaits your alert senses and open mind.

Understanding makes better enjoyment.

I need your input to improve on my effort to make the true nature of tea accessible for more people. Please feedback to me what you think about this book. Write to me at info@mingcha.com.hk, or at 1 Hoi Wan Street, #703, Quarry Bay, Hong Kong. Thank you for your support.